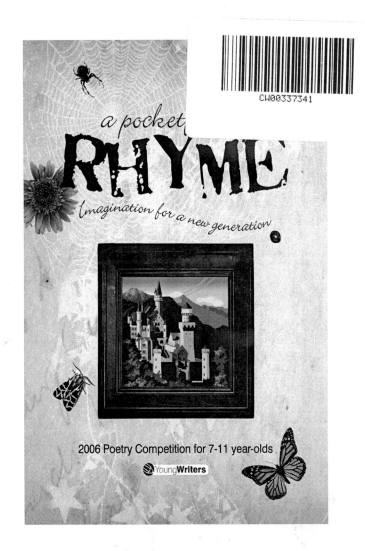

a pocket
RHYME
Imagination for a new generation

2006 Poetry Competition for 7-11 year-olds

YoungWriters

Cheshire Vol II
Edited by Allison Dowse

 Young**Writers**

First published in Great Britain in 2007 by:
Young Writers
Remus House
Coltsfoot Drive
Peterborough
PE2 9JX
Telephone: 01733 890066
Website: www.youngwriters.co.uk

SB ISBN 1 84602 737 3

Foreword

Young Writers was established in 1991 and has been passionately devoted to the promotion of reading and writing in children and young adults ever since. The quest continues today. Young Writers remains as committed to the nurturing of poetic and literary talent as ever.

This year's Young Writers competition has proven as vibrant and dynamic as ever and we are delighted to present a showcase of the best poetry from across the UK and in some cases overseas. Each poem has been selected from a wealth of *A Pocketful Of Rhyme* entries before ultimately being published in this, our fourteenth primary school poetry series.

Once again, we have been supremely impressed by the overall quality of the entries we have received. The imagination, energy and creativity which has gone into each young writer's entry made choosing the poems a challenging and often difficult but ultimately hugely rewarding task - the general high standard of the work submitted ensured this opportunity to bring their poetry to a larger appreciative audience.

We sincerely hope you are pleased with this final collection and that you will enjoy *A Pocketful Of Rhyme Cheshire Vol II* for many years to come.

Contents

Fraser Halson (10)   37
Charley Robson (11)   38
John Hay (10)   39
Jamie Yates (10)   40
Kyle Lunt (10)   41
Megan Roberts (7)   42
Joshua Jenner (7)   43
Ellis Robson (8)   44
Charlotte Stacey (7)   45
Warner Thomas Adshead (7)   46
Peter Hughes (7)   47
Cameron Atkinson (7)   48
Lewis Appleton-Jones (7)   49

Didsbury Road Primary School
Maya Devonald (10)   50
Abigail Pearce (10)   51
Dan Whitehead (10)   52
Rachel Lee (10)   53
Jacob Haynes (10)   54
Amila Kesedzic (10)   55
Sam Johnson (10)   56
Cian Rennie May (10)   57
Tom Daniel Hampson (11)   58
Alex Hartley (11)   59
Aisling Foley (10)   60
Jake Naylor (10)   61
Lucy Pilling (10)   62
Lauren Hemingway (10)   63
Annelise Bond (10)   64
Talith Walker (10)   65
Georgia Reed (10)   66
Daniel Furmidge (10)   67
Ben Watson (10)   68
Rachel Mason (10)   69
Naomi Bailey (10)   70
Rachel Cummings (10)   71
Molly Howden (10)   72
Harry Lyons (10)   73
Jack Roden (11)   74
Mark Jenkins (10)   75

Ethan Daniel Jude (8)   111
Tommy Ryan (8)   112
Dane Bramhall (9)   113
Sophie Davies (8)   114
Alex Anne Johnson (8)   115
Kaitlin Wells (9)   116
Amyleigh Lears (9)   117

St Basil's Primary School, Widnes
Brendan Conder (9)   118
Bethany Rowley (10)   119
Kate Parry (9)   120
Nichola Fraser (9)   121
Ryan Batty (9)   122
Matthew Harrison (9)   123
Keiron Gordon (9)   124
Louise Coleman (9)   125
Declan Shelley (9)   126
Regan Mullarkey (9)   127
Jamie Benson (9)   128
Ashley Giblin (9)   129
Jordan Jones (9)   130
Jamie Whittaker (7)   131
Andrew Lawler (7)   132
Jordan Batty (8)   133
Michael Hussey (7)   134
Matthew Bray (8)   135
Callum O'Connor (7)   136
Jenna McQuirk (7)   137
Marcus Dowd (8)   138
Mark Allen (7)   139
Olivia Hargreaves (7)   140
Terry Capes (8)   141
Olivia Alexander (7)   142
Amy Littler (7)   143

St Luke's CE Primary School, Warrington
Meghan O'Meara (8)   144
Gemma Baron (8)   145
Jake Knox (8)   146
Alex Cathie (8)   147

Lizzy Lever (8)   148
Daniel Hough (8)   149
Michael Donohue (8)   150
Megan Louise Simpson (9)   151
James Cathie (8)   152
Lewis Stones (8)   153
Dylan Lowe (9)   154
Kate Sutcliffe-Ralph (8)   155
Hayley Tait (10)   156
Edward Hanley (11)   157
Abigail Gibson (10)   158
Tommy Isherwood (9)   159
Ashley Hough (10)   160
Ashley Hughes (11)   161
Duncan Cathie (10)   162
Lorrna Allison (10)   163
Jessica Smart (10)   164
Alice Grix (10)   165
Laura Marston (10)   166
Alex Bradbury (10)   167
Beth Davies (10)   168
Alex Corcoran (10)   169
Annabelle Coveney (10)   170
Ben Graney (10)   171
Kathryn Gildart (10)   172
Jack Hamilton (10)   173
Aidan McMenemy (11)   174
Elle Hart (11)   175
Josh Taylor (10)   176
George Lythgoe (10)   177
Mark Harrison   178
Xaq Atkins (8)   179
Amy Bradford (7)   180

Sir John Offley CE (VC) Primary School
Josh Walley (10)   181
Jack Allport (10)   182
George Edwards (11)   183
Liam Jennings (10)   184
Eleasha Baddeley (10)   185
Bethany Lewis (11)   186

Keely Bagnall (10)	187
Elizabeth Courthold (10)	188
Hannah Beardmore (10)	189
Kate Valentine (10)	190
Eleni Caulcott (10)	191
Sophie Key (10)	192
Lucy Prall (10)	193
Thomas Hedley (10)	194
Dan Brown (10)	195
Jade Ellerton (10)	196
Tom Law (10)	197
Rebecca Machin (10)	198
Danielle Riley (10)	199

Tilston Parochial CE Primary School

Sam Scott (10)	200
Megan Adie (9)	201
Aimee Foden (10)	202
Ruby Doran (10)	203
Henry Delf-Rowlandson (10)	204
Andrew Ewins (10)	205
Liam Cork (8)	206
Lydia Ewins (8)	207
Liam Griffiths (11)	208
Lauren McGann (9)	209
Lizzie Hunter (10)	210

The Poems

Mystery Mayhem

They're faster than lightning,
Soft as a fluffy teddy,
Murkier than a lock,
Even twitchier than a snake.

Selfless as a chocolate bar,
Colourful as a present wrapper,
Tender and caring like a mother cat,
Smarter than an Oxford don.

Enthusiastic as a chimpanzee,
Sweeter than a candy cone,
Best people in the world.

Can be dumb as a dodo,
Cheesier than Swiss cheese,
Deafer than a nan.

I'll tell you it is only *the dinner ladies!*
Bet you cannot think who I am?

Charlie Lecossois (9)
Beechwood Primary School

Mr?

The deputy head of our school is:
As funny as the X Factor singers,
As kind as my grandma,
As sensible as a scientist,
As silly as a monkey,
Like a bright star in the sky.

As jolly as Father Christmas,
As hairy as a chimpanzee,
As clever as a calculator,
As cool as a kangaroo,
And his name is:

Mr Griffith!

Elise Potter (9)
Beechwood Primary School

A Teaching Assistant?

Her hair is as twisty as a curly fry,
She's as kind as my mum, (LOL),
She's as jolly as an elf,
She never gets numb.

As cool as a cucumber,
As jumpy as a jelly bean,
As sharp as a needle,
She's very, very keen.

As colourful as a rainbow,
As loud as a bull horn,
As shiny as tinfoil,
As crunchy as corn.

As fun as a video game
And this is her name:
Mrs Ashton.

Jonathan Ashton (9)
Beechwood Primary School

The Mysterious Secretary

The secretary

As kind as kind can be,
As funny as a monkey,
As tall as a tree.

The secretary

As nice as my mum,
As pretty as a rose,
As helpful as a computer.

The secretary

As shiny as a piece of glass,
As cheerful as laughter,
As fun as a funfair.

The secretary

As colourful as funny patterns,
As cool as ice cream,
As strict as an instructor
And her name is Mrs Lightfoot!

Alannah Garland (9)
Beechwood Primary School

The Mysterious Teacher

As calm as swaying trees,
As sweet as a toffee,
As clever as a computer,
Now which teacher is that?

As cool as a cloud,
As bright as a light bulb,
As helpful as a book,
Now which teacher is that?

As funny as a clown,
As grumpy as a grandma,
As cuddly as a teddy bear,
Now which teacher is that?

As disorganised as a cheeky monkey,
As friendly as a newborn puppy,
As happy as a hyena,
Now which teacher is that?

Can you guess which teacher this is?
Miss Medlicott!

Chloe McKnight (9)
Beechwood Primary School

The Tuneful Teacher

As musical as a bird,
As forgetful as Lewis,
As funny as a monkey,
As messy as a pup,
As mysterious as a secret,
As cracked as a cup,
Sometimes mad but not that bad,
As good as new,
As smart as a computer,
As jolly as a holiday,
As sweet as ice cream,
As fit as a fiddle,
As swift as a plane
And here is her name –

Mrs Wilks!

Lewis Smith (9)
Beechwood Primary School

Miss Horan

As nice as a kangaroo,
As calm as a sea,
As funny as Willy Wonka,
As polite as La La.

As happy as SpongeBob
As quiet as a rabbit,
As thin as a stick.

As tall as Peter Crouch,
As sweet as a toffee,
As helpful as a PC.

As clean as crystal water,
As organised as Miss Medlicott,
The teacher of Class 2.

Emma Hanshaw (9)
Beechwood Primary School

Mrs?

The head teacher of Beechwood School,
Is as cool as a kangaroo,
As small as a hill,
Everyone thinks she's brill,
As jolly as an elf,
She doesn't just care for herself,
As sweet as a lolly,
As colourful as a brolly,
As fun as a roller coaster,
As great as an ice cream,
As bright as the sun,
As loud as a scream,
As organised as my mum,
As helpful as a book,
She's definitely not dumb,
Like a fabulous thumbs up,
She is as tiny as a pin,
This teacher is Mrs Finn.

Emma Cowley (9)
Beechwood Primary School

Teacher Like The Eiffel Tower

The teacher of Class 3,
Is as tall as 3 of me,
As fun as a bouncy ball,
As organised as me,
As new as a pin,
As sneaky as a cat,
Lives as far away as Leicester,
I think she lives in Chester,
As friendly as a puppy,
As funny as money
And her name is Miss Brookes.

Adam Moore (9)
Beechwood Primary School

The Mysterious Dinner Lady

The dinner lady is
As kind as the world can be
As sweet as a toffee
As peaceful as Heaven
As huggable as a chimpanzee
As helpful as a computer
As small as me
As cool as ice
As much fun as a roller coaster
As cheerful as can be
Like a shiny star
As colourful as a rainbow
As loud as an audience
Like a tasty chocolate bar,
As calm as the ocean.

Who can this be?

Mrs Davis.

Laura Nield (9)
Beechwood Primary School

A T A Teacher

The teacher in Class 4 is:
As kind as a candy stick,
As pretty as a model,
As disorganised as my phone book.

The teacher in Class 4 is:
As nutty as a noodle,
As strict as a whistle,
As jumpy as a jellybean.

The teacher in Class 4 is:
As forgetful as a fish,
As smart as the Internet,
As warm as the Sahara Desert.

The teacher is Class 4 is:
As special as a secret,
As unusual as a good for nothing fruit,
As helpful as a handyman

And her name is *Mrs Kidd*.

Laura Cassidy (10)
Beechwood Primary School

Anger

Anger is like my head is going to burst like a fizzy lemonade bottle,
Anger sounds like a bomb hitting my head,
Anger tastes like rotten sour bananas and boiling hot chilli peppers,
Anger smells like smoke from a red-hot massive fire
And smelly, smelly socks with rotten cheese,
Anger feels like my muscles are going to burst,
What makes me really angry is when someone calls me names,
How I calm down is to go to sleep and when
I wake up - I will just forget about it.

Thomas Leonard (9)
Dane Bank Primary School

Anger

If anger was a colour, it would be red like fire
Coming from a burning house.

If anger was a sound, it would be like a balloon
Bursting when it's popped.

If anger was a taste, it would be like
Horrible green sprouts.

If anger was a smell, it would be like
A wet, soggy fish.

Anger feels like punching my wall,
What makes me angry is when
My little brother hits me.

What makes me calm down is when
I sit on my bed.

Daniel Lee (9)
Dane Bank Primary School

Anger

When I get angry, I go bright red,
Like a dragon breathing fire,
As if it's burning a house down.

It sounds like a train,
That has just skidded on a track,
As if it's about to crash!

When I am angry, it tastes like a hot pepper,
That's just come out of the oven,
As if it's pitch-black.

When I get angry, I feel like breaking something,
That's just been on a shelf for ages,
As if it's pitch-black.

I get angry when my sister annoys me by hurting me,
I calm down by punching a pillow ten times.

Alexandra Amy Faulkner (9)
Dane Bank Primary School

Anger

Anger is like a bull huffing and puffing,
Anger feels like running round in a circle,
Anger smells like boiled eggs,
Anger tastes like disgusting sprouts,
Anger feels like my blood vessels bursting,
Anger is like a ball hitting my head,
It makes me angry when my sister annoys me.

Rebecca Large (9)
Dane Bank Primary School

Anger

When I'm angry I am as red as a tomato,
Anger sounds like a lion roaring that has just been shot by a hunter,
If anger was a taste, it would taste like mud and dirt,
If anger was a smell, it would be like rotten fish,
Anger feels like taking a ride on a wild animal through a tornado,
What makes me mad is when Mum takes me off my game
When I have to go to bed,
I calm down by eating a salad sandwich and
Playing on my PS2.

Kane Hirons (9)
Dane Bank Primary School

Anger

Anger is the colour of a cherry bursting open,
Anger is like the sound of a kettle boiling,
Anger has got the taste of Brussels sprouts
Going down my throat,
Anger smells like lots of smelly socks,
Anger feels like someone hitting me across my face,
I get angry when my sister pushes me for no reason,
I calm down by eating ice cream.

Liam Garde (9)
Dane Bank Primary School

Anger

Anger is red like blood dripping down my body,
It smells like leaking petrol on the station floor,
It tastes like pollution in the air in the city,
If feels like a hard rock from the beach.

What makes me angry?
When people call me names and when my
Brothers and sisters wind me up,
How I calm down?
I bite my tongue and count to ten.

Abbie Walsh (10)
Dane Bank Primary School

Anger

Anger is red like blood dripping on a wall
In a horror film,
Anger sounds like someone being tortured by the Devil,
Anger feels like fire burning you to bits,
Anger tastes like toxic waste about to explode,
Anger smells like smoke and burnt rubber from a car bomb.

Jordan Sale (11)
Dane Bank Primary School

Anger

When the dogs are barking at night,
I'd love them to be out of sight,
Because they always make me go mad,
When I'm stressed, it makes me think of something bad.

What would anger look like as a colour?
All fiery with blazes of red, orange and yellow
And I wonder what anger would feel like?
All rough and pointy and sharp with nasty splinters.

Chloe Crooks (11)
Dane Bank Primary School

Anger

Anger is red like a volcano erupting in Lanzarote,
It smells like burning petrol in a deliberate fire,
It tastes like bitter lemon in my drink,
It looks like the war and all the people that have been shot,
It sounds like people crying because
Someone has died in their family,
It feels like some bulls charging at me,
What makes me angry is when I get
Left out of everything,
How I calm down is
I just go and chill on my bed.

Joe Sumner (10)
Dane Bank Primary School

Anger

Anger is a black bull charging at a red sheet,
Anger sounds like a bomb booming on a house,
Anger tastes like vegetables especially broccoli,
Anger smells like a bonfire on Bonfire Night,
Anger feels like revenge on someone.

Ryan Gooch (9)
Dane Bank Primary School

Anger

Anger is jet-black like a closed down mine,
It smells like rotten fish at the side of the river,
It tastes like lime and lemon mixed together,
It feels like World War II,
It sounds like a baby screeching in pain,
What makes me angry is when people
Leave me out and shout at me for no reason,
How can I calm down?
I punch my pillow.

Amy Boslem (10)
Dane Bank Primary School

Anger

Anger is like a red balloon starting to pop and turn black,
I can hear anger rushing right through my body to the check point,
I can taste anger in my taste buds like green beans,
I can smell anger right to the very beginning,
Anger feels like my head is going to burst,
My little brother makes me angry,
I can calm down on my PlayStation.

James Holland (9)
Dane Bank Primary School

Anger

Anger is blue like a bunch of blueberries being
Squashed by a little boy stamping on them,
Anger smells like lasagne that's been there
For half a year,
Anger tastes like flat Coke and I drink it by mistake
When I get up,
Anger feels like steam coming out of an
Old-fashioned train that is rushing to the next station,
Anger sounds like a screaming mouse
Being eaten by a tomcat.

Rebekah Daniels (10)
Dane Bank Primary School

Anger

If anger was a colour, it would be like flaming hot fire,
If anger was a sound, it would be like rough roaring sea,
If anger was a taste, it would be like hot spicy chicken
                                        burning my mouth!

I get angry when I lose my purse and my Princess Max,
I calm down by forgetting about them, then they turn up.

Molly Olivia Keane (7)
Dane Bank Primary School

Anger

Anger is red like the sun burning up in the sky,
Anger sounds like a dog growling so loud inside my head,
Anger tastes like strong onions and I need lots of water,
Anger smells like smoke from a fiery dragon flying in the sky,
Anger feels like a firework exploding inside me,
I get angry when my brother messes up my stuff,
I calm down by going in my room and closing my eyes.

Hannah Rachael Costin (10)
Dane Bank Primary School

Anger

When I am angry, the colour of my cheeks
Is red like a fire in a burning building,
When I am angry, the sound I make is
A screaming sound like a little girl getting kidnapped,
When I am angry the taste in my mouth is
Like pencil sharpeners and spit coming out of my mouth,
The smell is like bad breath,
The thing that makes me really angry
Is when my brother really annoys me and
I calm myself down by having a quiet time by myself.

Yasmine Sarah Tait (10)
Dane Bank Primary School

Anger

Anger is black like the sky at night,
Anger is loud like a rocket bursting,
Anger is gross like eating snails,
Anger is smoky like burnt bacon,
When my nephew hits me I get angry,
I calm him down by tickling him.

Sam Butterfield (8)
Dane Bank Primary School

Anger

Anger is black like the big night sky,
Anger is loud like a scream of a girl,
Anger is sour like sour sea water,
Anger is stinky like wet mud in a forest,
I get angry when Fraser goes on my PlayStation 2,
I calm down by going to sleep.

Rory Halson (8)
Dane Bank Primary School

Anger

Anger is red like fire bursting hot,
Anger is sharp like a dog barking loud,
Anger is salty like Sprite,
Anger is burning like smoke out of the chimney,
I get angry when my brother takes over my games,
I calm down by going to my bedroom for 10 minutes
And lying on my bed.

Calvin Alexander (8)
Dane Bank Primary School

Anger

Anger is red like fireworks when they blast up into the air,
Anger is loud like Mum shouting me down to get my breakfast,
Anger is a taste like burnt toast for my breakfast,
Then my sister calms me down by playing with me.

Luke Auld (8)
Dane Bank Primary School

Anger

Anger is blue like the sea when it crashes against the rocks,
Anger sounds like a roar of a tiger,
Anger tastes like snot out of my nose,
Anger smells like a pair of socks that stink.

Oliver Mooney (8)
Dane Bank Primary School

Anger

Anger is red like blood in your body,
Anger is loud and bumpy like having a disco,
Anger is a taste like a hot sweet burning my mouth,
Anger smells like smelly green socks,
That you have been wearing all day,
I get angry when my sister punches me!

Lauren Jaye Ashbee (8)
Dane Bank Primary School

Anger

Anger is black like a black panther leaping in the jungle,
Anger is like a black panther growling, guarding its family,
Anger tastes like Fanta when I am not in the mood for it,
Anger smells like water bubbling in a pan,
I get angry when I make a model
And someone knocks it down and it took me ages,
I calm down by going on my PS2 games.

Thomas Wolstenholme (9)
Dane Bank Primary School

Anger

When I have an argument with my mum,
I feel hot like a kettle boiling,
All I can hear in my mind is people
Yelling at each other,
I can taste sour lemon juice trickling round my mouth,
I feel like black smoke is suffocating me,
I just want to walk out of the door
And never come back,
I cuddle my teddy, go down to my mum,
Say sorry and give her a hug.

Grace Keane (10)
Dane Bank Primary School

Anger

Anger is red like a fire burning down the house,
It is black like a blackbird eating all of the crops,
Anger tastes bitter like a freshly picked orange,
It tastes like a hot chilli forced into my mouth,
Anger smells like smoke that has come off a bonfire,
It smells like a wet dog that has just come out of the rain,
Anger sounds like music booming out loud,
It sounds like the screeching sound when a
Knife and fork are scraped together,
Anger feels like I am going to explode,
It feels like I am on fire, then I burn to death,
I get angry when I get called names for no reason,
To calm me down I go to another place and count to 10.

Fraser Halson (10)
Dane Bank Primary School

Anger

Anger feels like lava burning inside me,
Anger looks like a volcano erupting over a city,
Anger sounds like a bomb exploding in the middle of a town,
Anger tastes like burning toast, crumbling in my mouth,
I feel angry when my mum and dad shout at me for no reason,
I calm down by punching my wardrobe, then I count to ten.

Charley Robson (11)
Dane Bank Primary School

Anger

Anger is red like lava flowing through the city,
It tastes bitter like a lemon getting crushed into my mouth,
Anger smells like burnt sausages in the cooker,
Anger feels boiling like putting your hand in a bonfire,
Anger sounds like music put on full volume
And to calm down!
Go to a peaceful place and count to ten.

John Hay (10)
Dane Bank Primary School

Anger

Anger is blue like the current pulling
A drowning man round the sea,
Anger tastes like a cigarette even though I don't smoke,
Anger smells like a burning house with people screaming for help,
Anger sounds like people running for their lives because of shooting.

Jamie Yates (10)
Dane Bank Primary School

Anger

Anger is red like a dagger covered in blood,
I see lava pouring out of a volcano and
It is burning the city down,
I hear screeching like a dying bird in its nest,
I can taste the sour milk that's left out
On the kitchen table overnight,
I can feel the sweat dripping off my face
Like a steaming kettle,
I smell the rotting fish in the polluted ocean.

I get angry when my mum sends me to bed,
I calm down by sitting on my sofa and watching
Television in my room.

Kyle Lunt (10)
Dane Bank Primary School

Anger

If anger was a colour,
It would be red like hot fire from a dragon's mouth,
If anger was a sound,
It would be like a whirlwind zooming around,
If anger was a taste,
It would taste like a rotten tomato being cooked,
I get angry when my friends come round for tea,
My little brother comes and wrecks the game and annoys me,
So I turn around, I count to twenty,
Then I make friends and carry on playing.

Megan Roberts (7)
Dane Bank Primary School

Anger

If anger was a colour,
It would be red like devils spinning round my head,
If anger was a sound,
It would be a bomb at night,
If anger was a taste,
It would be blood running down my throat.

Joshua Jenner (7)
Dane Bank Primary School

Anger

If anger was a colour,
It would be black like a wild animal,
If anger was a sound,
It would be like a T-Rex fighting for its prey roaring 'Rooaarrr!'
If anger was a taste,
It would be like a pie with fish guts in it,
When I get angry, I kick my sister and
I get sent to my bedroom.

Ellis Robson (8)
Dane Bank Primary School

Anger

If anger was a colour, the colour would be red like
A loud firework in the sky,
If anger was a sound, it would be a car starting to go,
If anger was a taste, it would be a salted bean!

I get angry when my sister bites me.

I calm down by my sister saying sorry.

Charlotte Stacey (7)
Dane Bank Primary School

Anger

If anger was a colour, it would be red,
Like a burning fire,
If it was a sound, it would be a like a steam train,
If anger had a taste, it would taste like burning chicken,
I calm down by counting to 1000!

Warner Thomas Adshead (7)
Dane Bank Primary School

Anger

If anger was a colour,
It would be fiery red!
If anger was a sound,
It would be a windy jet engine,
If anger was a taste,
It would be a spicy curry,
I get angry when it is rainy
And I have got to stay inside,
Anger makes me go burning inside!
I calm down by taking 3 deep breaths!

Peter Hughes (7)
Dane Bank Primary School

Anger

If anger was a colour, it would be red as lava,
If anger was a sound, it would be like dynamite,
If anger was a taste, it would be hot peppers,
I get angry when I lose at football,
I calm down when I score!

Cameron Atkinson (7)
Dane Bank Primary School

Anger

If anger was a colour,
It would be black like a hurricane,
If it had a sound,
It would be thunder in a storm,
Its taste would be black pepper on pizza,
I get angry when my sister comes into my room,
I calm down when she goes out.

Lewis Appleton-Jones (7)
Dane Bank Primary School

Storms

The clouds scream and shout
And weep and cry,
Making a great deal of water
Fall from the sky.

The lightning bolts reach
With its huge great arms,
Then cackles at the people
That are waiting till it calms.

The wind whistled
His favourite tune,
Then sneezed
And everybody wished it was June.

But then someone came
To stop the storm's fun,
It always has a smile
And it was the sun.

Maya Devonald (10)
Didsbury Road Primary School

The Dishwasher

Hiding under the workbench,
Hunched in a small place,
A one-eyed, shock-mouthed brown face,
Staring boldly at the kitchen,
Waiting patiently to gobble dirty greasy plates.
Its mouth yawning open, then closing slowly,
Swallows hard.
It chews rudely slurping and splashing its dinner,
Its tummy hums and rumbles and digests its food,
Opening its massive mouth again,
It spits the bones out politely then rests.

Abigail Pearce (10)
Didsbury Road Primary School

The Tree

The tree sat there withered, pleading for water,
Its feet clung onto the ground, hoping to find water,
Its arms were reaching out, trying to get water,
Its face had sprouted a beard, but still it needed water,
Its eyes never looked just at one place, all they wanted was water,
Its skin was peeling off and wrinkly, due to the lack of water,
Its nose had long not worked, it desperately needed water,
The ground beneath it fell away, rocks clung against rocks,
The tree knew it had no hopes to live.

Dan Whitehead (10)
Didsbury Road Primary School

The Sun

The sun smiles down onto the people on their holiday,
They look up and smile back and think of a hot spot ahead,
The sun laughs over the giggles of the trees,
As the car drives past under the hot happy sun.

Rachel Lee (10)
Didsbury Road Primary School

Hallowe'en

Hallowe'en is a time of great fear,
Bats hide in the shadows far and near,
Pumpkins cackle from the window sill,
As witches bend over a cauldron in the abandoned mill,
Children go from door to door,
Trick or treating, sweets galore!
The sweets crouch down and wait,
Not so sure this will be their fate,
But what the children don't know is round the bend,
Might very well be their end,
So take caution on Hallowe'en
And if unwanted, don't be seen . . .

Jacob Haynes (10)
Didsbury Road Primary School

Weather

The rain spits at everything, everywhere,
The houses howl as the wind hits them,
Sun smiles at all the children playing at the beach,
Thunder and lightning roar at everything they see.

The hailstones scream as they hit everything,
All the snowflakes have a different pattern,
They all giggle as the snow is rolled up
And thrown into the air.

Amila Kesedzic (10)
Didsbury Road Primary School

Dancing With Fire

Flames prance and dance around
It is yellow like a traffic light
And when it goes out, it falls to the ground
What a sight.

The fire clicks its fingers and out come sparks
They fly or they drop
Sometimes you can see sharks
It goes out and then sometimes makes a smiley face.

The fire flutters and flies up to the trees leaves
The wood falls and burns the grass
And the ash can sometimes burn all the trees
The fire finishes his show and does his last dance.

Sam Johnson (10)
Didsbury Road Primary School

Night-Time

Night-time crawls in as the sun goes to sleep,
Night-time doesn't smile,
He stares into nothing.

Night-time is a dark figure and wears a black cloak,
Night-time hovers in front of the sun,
As the moon comes out to dance.

Cian Rennie May (10)
Didsbury Road Primary School

The Sea

The sea is salty and the water strong,
People who underestimate it are very wrong,
The moon controls the sea and can make it rough or friendly,
But when the weather is rough, it can be very deadly,
The sea can swallow humans and ships,
It jumps up and tries to reach fingertips.

Tom Daniel Hampson (11)
Didsbury Road Primary School

The Town

The very big building stands tall and proud over all the others
And the sea is boasting how blue it is,
The clock peers over and watches the town from a great height,
The mountains grow colder every day
And the boats float lonely on the silvery face of the sea.

Alex Hartley (11)
Didsbury Road Primary School

Messing Around On The Lilo

Messing around on the lilo,
Sabrina, Laura and me,
Falling into the deepness of the pool,
Sabrina, Laura and me,
Messing around on the lilo,
Sabrina, Laura and me,
Floating around looking up at the sky,
Sabrina, Laura and me,
Messing around on the lilo,
Sabrina, Laura and me,
Splashing each other for hours and hours,
Sabrina, Laura and me,
Messing around on the lilo,
Sabrina, Laura and me,
Flinging ourselves all over the lilo,
Sabrina, Laura and me,
Messing around on the lilo,
Sabrina, Laura and me,
Making bridges out of the lilo,
Sabrina, Laura and me,
Messing around on the lilo,
Sabrina, Laura and me,
Having fun all day long,
Sabrina, Laura and me.

Aisling Foley (10)
Didsbury Road Primary School

The Great Storm

The house gripped onto the ground as the tornado rushed past,
The wind howled like a werewolf at full moon,
The sun tried to peer through the black storm,
The rain clouds cried onto the beach,
The waves jumped onto the beach,
The fire ran across the trees' branches.

Jake Naylor (10)
Didsbury Road Primary School

Plants

P lease don't pick me,
L eave me to grow
A nd I will not let you down,
N othing will stop me,
T o do something extraordinary,
S o leave me to grow and I will be your friend.

Lucy Pilling (10)
Didsbury Road Primary School

Fire

Fire crackling,
Spitting and hissing,
Whispering out of tune.

Fire dances,
Prances and
Warms our toes.

Fire sits in
The hearth
Desperate to escape
From its small space.

Fire wants to scream
With anger worse than death.

He wouldn't mind if you fainted
Because you were scared of him,
He wouldn't dare give a helping hand!

Lauren Hemingway (10)
Didsbury Road Primary School

The Boat

The water danced around the boat,
The deckchairs laughed up at the sun,
The glistening pool on the top deck,
Lay still watching the clouds run by.

The cabin's portholes peered out,
To see the stars showing off their light,
The boat is asleep except the engine,
The engine keeps roaring
As though complaining of her travels.

Annelise Bond (10)
Didsbury Road Primary School

The Cat

The miaow of the cat, echoed through the hall,
She peered round to see who had heard her call,
Then she crawled into her hideout, feeling safe and warm,
She sat and waited for the response of something, but
There was no noise, not even the sound of her own breath.
Could she be dreaming or could she be abandoned?
But when she settled down to sleep,
She heard footsteps, were these human?
Of course they were but she seemed not to care . . .
All she wanted to know was that something or somebody was there.

Talith Walker (10)
Didsbury Road Primary School

Beautiful Garden

Leaves twisting around, strangling the wooden beams,
Plants struggling for space,
Pathway weaving through all the growing plants,
Where will it lead?

Pink flowers sing in the bright sky,
Sunshine peeking through the trellis feeding the plants,
Red, pink, green and yellow plants,
Staring at each other admiring their colours.

Georgia Reed (10)
Didsbury Road Primary School

Tree

I weep in the dying sun as I glare up at the purple sky,
I sleep tight when an owl comes and lands on me,
I boil in rage,
So I make my act and swing my branches and
Laugh at the helpless creature.
I fall asleep once again to have sweet dreams about tomorrow.
When morning comes I am not so happy to say,
A bird lands on my branches, to begin the day,
After I shooed the bird away,
I decided to make my leaves whisper in the wind.

Daniel Furmidge (10)
Didsbury Road Primary School

The Wave

The boats in the Pacific sea
Are nearing their doom,
As they say,
There's a high wind today,
But they must sail, either way.

It's getting choppy,
But peace is still theirs,
As the winds fly
And they eat their pies,
The waves engulf them to their end.

The wave puts on its evil smile
And looks at its feast,
1 boat, 2 boats, 3,
All tickle his appetite
And he tucks in.

There is a panic,
The wave is engulfing them,
Intimidating his meal,
Cleansing his smile,
The boats are ripped into him.

The boats are ripped on the surface,
They have no choice but to retreat,
There is none left,
But they have no choice,
As they have no chance.

As the wave keeps its wicked smile,
It goes away,
Leaving the boats,
In the calm,
Thinking about nothing,
Left alone in the sea.

Ben Watson (10)
Didsbury Road Primary School

The Solar System

The sky is silent,
Not a whisper to be heard,
Only twinkling stars can be seen,
When you look above,
Only the moon stares back at you yawning,
The shooting star sprints about,
From planet to planet,
The sun waits patiently to rise for the day
And the rocket passing says, 'Hello!'

Rachel Mason (10)
Didsbury Road Primary School

The Blustery Night

Two old oaks in a graveyard stood,
Solemn and sombre,
Though ancient and knobbly energy still floods,
On nights that are still, they are limp and lack lustre,
They are waiting for winds that will blow and will bluster.

Winds from the north hurried about,
Lifting their arm like branches and making the trees shout,
With fingers entwined they bow and they bend,
Their leaves whistle and fall whilst
A message the trees send.

With laugher and joy and hope in our hearts,
Me and my friend will never part.

Naomi Bailey (10)
Didsbury Road Primary School

Fire

As the trees screamed in the dark, dark night,
Fire laughed louder and set them alight.

Birds from all corners fled with fear,
As flames broke out far and near.

Squirrels swung away up through the trees,
Racing fire who was as fast as the breeze.

Crackling and sniggering was fire's sound,
As he roared and jeered and he danced all around.

'I've won! I've won! There's no doubt,
Just look at your forest, there's fire all about.'

When all seemed lost and fire had won,
Out came the rain and the fire was done.

Rachel Cummings (10)
Didsbury Road Primary School

The Guitar – Haiku

It screams as it plays
Screeches in the summer sun
Playing lots of tunes.

Molly Howden (10)
Didsbury Road Primary School

The Eiffel Tower

Millions of screws and bolts,
Stacked high into the sky,
People climbing right up,
To view all of Paris.

Lit up at night,
Big tower, big fright,
Stacked right up into the sky,
Reaching clouds, it is very high.

Elevator shooting up,
To reach the top,
Go to Paris and have a go,
It's good.

Harry Lyons (10)
Didsbury Road Primary School

Cars

The car raced along like a silver bullet
Being shot from a gun,
Wheels turning, speeding and racing,
Twisting and turning as it takes the bends
And the beautiful engine humming its beautiful song.

Jack Roden (11)
Didsbury Road Primary School

Monster House

Ghosts cackle and zombies fight,
They all come out in the dead of night,
Floorboards moan,
Doors groan,
Frankenstein wants to play,
Please just get away!
You've left the formula,
To kill evil Dracula in the car!

Mark Jenkins (10)
Didsbury Road Primary School

The Secret Tin

This is the cupboard like red juicy lips,
Full of chocolate and sugary sweets.

This is the girl like really hard iron,
Who has beady eyes like a shooting cannonball.

This is the mum who's strict and mean,
Who shouts to the girl 'I'm not very keen!' (On sweets)

This is the girl who steals the tin,
Takes it up to her room
And scoffs it all (in her mouth).

Megan Motler (10)
Didsbury Road Primary School

Barbados

The sweet smell of the coconut trees' breath,
The sea horses are galloping madly like they are actually horses,
The sandy towel trying to sneeze off the sand that lays dead
on the towel.

The sky so blue it is like my brother's eyes,
The crab scattered across the smooth silk sand
That lies beneath its tiny feet,
The sun beds are sinking into the sand
Like a woman lying in a mud bath.

Joshua Robert Antony Welch (10)
Didsbury Road Primary School

Sun And The Moon

The sun shines bright,
As the birds are humming,
The moon stands out light,
As the stars are coming.

The moon is coated in white,
As the sun shows the light
And as the rays of the sun suddenly die,
Finally the moon comes by.

The colour is pretty in the twilight,
As the vanilla skies stand out,
The sun is suddenly gone,
As the moon comes out.

Stephanie Baars
Didsbury Road Primary School

The Cars

The car drives as fast as the wind,
The car zooms through the road,
The engine makes a thundering sound,
The wheels spin as fast as a cheetah,
The shining light on the car could break the darkness,
The car colour could be as yellow as the sunshine.

Yasser Hamid
Didsbury Road Primary School

Dogs

The children jump like a puppy,
They run like a dog,
They fetch kicked balls like a puppy,
They play with you like a dog,
They roll over like a puppy.

Chanta Henry (10)
Didsbury Road Primary School

Sweets

The Chewits coughed as they walked into the cupboard,
The Haribo skipped off a shelf into the child's hand,
The Refresher screamed as it got chewed up by a child,
The lemon sherbets tickled the man's throat.

Emma Scott (10)
Didsbury Road Primary School

Personification Poem

The sea waved as the boat smiled,
A car shouted as it walked off,
My bike gave me a piggy-back as I got on it,
The curtains danced as the wind tickled them
And the moon slept until the dawn woke up.

Maria Hussain (10)
Didsbury Road Primary School

Coughing Cars

When a car coughs it runs down the street,
Its shiny bumper eyes people as they walk,
The car screams like mad as it zooms down the motorway.

Zayeem Nehal (11)
Didsbury Road Primary School

The Haunted House

In the dead of night, the haunted house
Awaited its first victim,
In the window, the pumpkin laughed.
The spider crept up to the man and caught its prey,
The house snapped his jaws as its first victim stepped inside.

Ryan Burton (10)
Didsbury Road Primary School

The Black Horse

Sir Billy was silly,
So silly they say,
He rode a black horse along the bay,
All through the day and into the night,
He rode a black horse with all his might.

Caitlin Lynch (9)
High Legh Primary School

Animals

There's bats with hats
And rats on mats.

Dogs with logs
And warthogs stuck in bogs.

Sharks stay in the dark,
Larks live in Noah's Ark.

Pigs wearing wigs
And earwigs doing jigs.

Sheep in heaps,
Their skins for keeps.

All these animals as you can see,
Are very, very different from you and me!

Bethan Catchpole (8)
High Legh Primary School

Down At The Swamp

Down at the swamp at the end of the day,
There was a crocodile having a play,
He wriggled and jiggled all up to his mum,
Under hot African sun.

Down at the waterhole close to dawn,
A tiger cub was having a yawn.

He drank and drank until he felt sick,
After that he chased a stick.

Down at the opening close today,
A lioness was hunting her prey,
Soon another lion killed her boar,
The lioness let out a tremendous *roar!*

David Marshall (9)
High Legh Primary School

Dinosaurs

As the sun lights the horizon
And the mist begins to clear,
What shapes can you see?
What noises can you hear?

Some of them have huge long necks
And some have giant jaws,
So come into the swampland
And let's meet the dinosaurs.

One is as little as a chicken,
But please don't be too hasty,
Although it may be chicken-sized,
It's not very tasty.

One is not very clever,
Cos its brain is very small,
But why does it need to be clever,
When it's twenty-five feet tall?

One is the triceratops,
Who says, 'How do you do?'
It's got these three horns on its head
And it looks really ugly too.

One is big and strong,
But it's always pleased to meet you,
Because its giant gaping jaws,
Are very keen to eat you.

So now you have met the dinosaurs,
What a fierce bunch,
Some of them would really like,
To eat you for their lunch.

But it is time to say goodbye now,
So away we will softly creep,
Cos even great big dinosaurs,
Have to go to sleep.

Zaynah Arub Ahmed (8)
High Legh Primary School

My Box Is A Sports Box

Inside my box lies a pitch of green,
Outside my box stands a country's team,
On top of my box dives a goalkeeper to save,
Under my box tackles the player to get the ball,
Far away from my box walk the fans that cheer,
Near my box stands a stadium nearby.

Tommy Atherton (8)
Mansfield Primary School

My Box Is A Toy Box

Inside my box is a dancing toy,
Near my box is a dancing dog,
Over my box is a ballerina,
Under my box is a zooming car,
By the side of my box is a talking dog.

Brittany Elwell (7)
Mansfield Primary School

My Box Is A Toy Box

Over my box lies a cuddly teddy,
Inside my box rolls a bouncy ball,
On my box jumps a big bear,
Near my box lies a big soft toy,
On top of my box skips a big doll,
Far away from my box stands a soldier.

Natasha Edwards (7)
Mansfield Primary School

My Box Is A Racing Box

Inside my box
Is a racing car.

Outside my box
Is a racing bike.

Near my box
Is a black and white flag.

On top of my box
Curves a racing track.

Shaun O'Regan (7)
Mansfield Primary School

The Yellow Tang

I am a yellow tang,
Swimming in the deep blue sea,
I am as yellow as a sunflower
And as bright as can be.
Swimming through the rocks all day,
Is such great fun,
Lots of other brightly coloured fishes,
Swimming by my side,
But when the deep-sea divers come
We all begin to hide,
This is our home in the deep blue sea
And this is where we want to be!

Anneka Mulvey (9)
Our Lady's Catholic Primary School

Hallowe'en

We are the leaves blowing everywhere,
I am the wind rushing through your hair,
She is the moon giving you a fright,
On this dark, dark, Hallowe'en night,
Hallowe'en, Hallowe'en, Hallowe'en!

We are the witches plotting a spell,
I am the ghost that fell, fell, fell,
She is the owl saying tu-whit, tu-whoo,
The vampire scares the life out of you,
Hallowe'en, Hallowe'en, Hallowe'en.

We are the clocks running out of time,
I am the coldness shivering your spine,
She is the wolf howling in the moonlight,
On this dark, dark, Hallowe'en night,
Hallowe'en, Hallowe'en, Hallowe'en.

Kate Mary Livesey (11)
Our Lady's Catholic Primary School

Abbie

My hair is as straight as a ruler,
My eyes are as blue as the sky,
My nose is like a button,
My smile is like a cheeky monkey.

I'm as bubbly as champagne,
I laugh like a chimpanzee,
I'm as sneaky as a snake.

I am a panther when I run,
I chomp like a crocodile,
I'm a dancing queen,
The best you've ever seen.

Abbie Murphy (11)
Our Lady's Catholic Primary School

All About Me

My hair is like a shining star in the air,
My eyes are as brown as a chocolate button,
I am as strong as a buffalo,
My neck is as big as a giraffe's,
I'm as talkative as a parrot.

I love to make a joke,
I am as bright as a button,
I am as shy as a fox.

I sing like Frank Sinatra, Dean Martin and Sammy Davis Junior,
I play football like Ronaldo,
I play rugby like Lee Briers.

James Whibley (10)
Our Lady's Catholic Primary School

My Snake

My snake is a skipping rope being waved on the ground,
Making a loud, hissing sound.

She is multicoloured, like the rainbow in the sky,
Above all the clouds moving slowly by.

Her tail rattles like a baby's soft lullaby,
As she gently slithers by.

She is as long as a river,
Winding on and on,
One minute she's there,
The next minute, she's gone.

Ciara O'Callaghan (10)
Our Lady's Catholic Primary School

The Cat

I saw a cat run across my garden,
Her eyes were as blue as sapphires,
Her ears were as pointed as a sharp pencil,
Her fur was as smooth as a silk scarf.

The cat ran as fast as the wind along the wall,
She stopped and jumped and landed on my ball,
Then bounced away and curled up small,
As I ran to watch her from the window in the hall.

She looked so cold, she gave me goosebumps,
Then looked at me with eyes as big as saucers
And miaowed as loud as a car alarm,
So I gave her some milk, I got from the farm.

Joshua Leah (11)
Our Lady's Catholic Primary School

I Wish I Was . . .

I wish I was a butterfly,
Flying high in the sky.

I wish I was a monkey,
Swinging from tree to tree.

I wish I was a giraffe,
That would be a great laugh.

I wish I was a penguin,
Waddling on the ice, that would be nice.

I wish I was a bee,
Buzzing everywhere, making sweet honey.

I wish I was a dolphin,
Swimming in the sea,
But for now I'll have to be me.

Antonia Swann (10)
Our Lady's Catholic Primary School

My Pet Hamster Joey

I bought a hamster from Pets At Home
And bought him a big cage all of his own.

My hamster is beige and white . . .
And he runs as wild as a chipmunk about the house at night.

His eyes are as red as a rose
And he has a cute little button nose.

My hamster is white as snow and looks like a fluff ball,
But when he stands up on his back legs, he looks very tall.

He loves to run wild on his wheel at night
And when I open his cage door, I give him quite a fright.

He is as sneaky as a fox
And he gives us quite a lot of shocks.

His favourite food is rice,
He loves it, he thinks it's very nice.

Although he's grown old,
I know deep down inside, he is still strong and bold.

And although he has died,
I know he died with pride.

Alice Cornelia (10)
Our Lady's Catholic Primary School

Victorian Days

Back in the day,
The teachers made the children pay,
Being whacked by the cane,
Gave the children a lot of pain.

Victoria was a pest,
She never was the best,
Wearing filthy old rags,
Made the children very drab.

Dancing round the May Pole,
Gave the children a lot of joy,
Especially with a girl and a boy.

Working in the factories,
Made the children sad,
But seeing their families,
Made the children glad.

James Guy (10)
Our Lady's Catholic Primary School

Victorian Poem

Children in Victorian times were working down the mines,
Victorian school rules were so mean,
Giving children the cane was such a pain.

Children in Victorian times were forced up the chimney
Although they didn't want to go,
They were up and down like a yo-yo,
Victorian school rules were so mean,
No elbows on the table, not even to write a fable.

Boys in Victorian times working at the factories,
Didn't like their working hours,
Victorian times were *mean!*

Joseph John Oakes (10)
Our Lady's Catholic Primary School

The Guinea Pig

He scurries along, can't be caught,
Silky fur, as soft as a petal,
His cabbage-cutting teeth are blades munching,
As his stubby sausage tail hangs lifeless,
His squeak, like an alien, calls to the others
And they play until the sun goes down.

Leanne Gemma White (9)
Our Lady's Catholic Primary School

Electric Neons

We swim together as tight as sardines,
We are as fast as leopards,
We are ice-blue and blood-red,
We shimmer and shine like silver hubcaps,
We are as sneaky as lions,
We are electric neons!

Daniel Hazell (10)
Our Lady's Catholic Primary School

Callum

(Based on 'The Writer of this Poem' by Roger McGough)

Is faster than a cheetah,
As tall as a tree,
As thin as can be.

As handsome as can be,
Has eyes like a conker,
As strong as a lion,
As smart as can be.

Callum,
Never ceases to amaze,
He is one in a million billion,
Or so the poem says.

Callum O'Callaghan (8)
Our Lady's Catholic Primary School

Mrs Nulty

Mrs Nulty is the best,
She always puts us to the test,
She always says number 4,
She always sends us out the door,
Always happy, never sad,
Makes me feel very glad,
Gives a smile and a cuddle,
If we feel in any trouble.

Shelley Brocklehurst (8)
Our Lady's Catholic Primary School

A Day At The Zoo

The elephants went for a walk
And the giraffes were having a talk
The bats were hanging upside down,
Then they were flying around,
The horses were rolling around in the hay,
Then they were saying neigh,
The water hogs were swimming in the lake,
While the owner cleaned up the dirty hay with his rake.

Georgia Taylor (8)
Our Lady's Catholic Primary School

Jamie

Is funnier than a clown
And never pulls a frown,
As fast as a cheetah
And can jump a metre,
He really is the best
And he always makes a mess,
He is as cunning as a leopard
And always makes an effort.

Jamie Solan (8)
Our Lady's Catholic Primary School

Fred Fish . . .

(Based on 'The Writer of this Poem' by Roger McGough)

Shinier than silver
As quick as a shark
As wet as can be
As orange as an orange
As slippery as an eel
As greedy as a whale
As active as a bee
Fred Fish,
Never ceases to amaze
He is one in a million billion
Or so the poem says.

Charlie Rowles (8)
Our Lady's Catholic Primary School

Philip – Haiku

Is really funny
Is as spiky as a bush
Taller than a tree.

Philip O'Brien (9)
Our Lady's Catholic Primary School

My Hamster James

My hamster James,
Likes to train animals for the
Olympic Games,
My hamster James,
Likes to set stuff up in flames,
My hamster James,
Drinks from the drains,
My hamster James,
Gains his power from his brains!

Ethan Daniel Jude (8)
Our Lady's Catholic Primary School

My Mum – Haiku

She is very cute
Lovely as a red, red rose
I love her so much.

Tommy Ryan (8)
Our Lady's Catholic Primary School

Shelley . . .

(Based on 'The Writer of this Poem' by Roger McGough)

Is prettier than a butterfly,
As cool as a cucumber,
As happy as can be.

As sharp as a pin,
Taller than a tree,
Prouder than a peacock,
As silly as a clown.

Shelley never ceases to amaze,
She's one in a million billion,
Or so the poem says.

Dane Bramhall (9)
Our Lady's Catholic Primary School

Sophie
(Inspired by 'The Writer of this Poem' by Roger McGough)

The writer of this poem is . . .
As clever as a tick,
As blind as a bat,
As white as a sheet,
As small as a mouse,
As fierce as a lion,
As fast as lightning,
As quiet as a cat.

Sophie Davies (8)
Our Lady's Catholic Primary School

Shelley

(Based on 'The Writer of this Poem' by Roger McGough)

Shelley is
Prettier than a princess,
As silly as a clown,
As kind as can be.

As cute as a kitten,
As cuddly as a teddy,
As warm as toast,
As small as a mouse.

Shelley
Never ceases to amaze
She is one in a million billion
(Or so the poem says).

Alex Anne Johnson (8)
Our Lady's Catholic Primary School

Frankie

(Based on 'The Writer of this Poem' by Roger McGough)

Frankie
Is funnier than a monkey,
As pretty as a flower,
As fast as can be.

As warm as toast,
As clean as a chemist shop,
As small as a mouse,
As tricky as a fib.

Frankie
Never ceases to amaze
She is one in a million billion
(Or so the poem says!)

Kaitlin Wells (9)
Our Lady's Catholic Primary School

Year 4/5

(Based on 'The Writer of this Poem' by Roger McGough)

Are smarter than a teacher,
As strong as a wrestler,
As small as can be.

As cute as kittens,
As warm as toast,
As cuddly as teddies,
As cool as cucumbers.

Y4/5,
Never cease to amaze,
We are one in a million billion,
(Or so the poem says!)

Amyleigh Lears (9)
Our Lady's Catholic Primary School

Dinosaurs

Dinosaurs' feet are the like falling asteroids
Hitting the ground.

Dinosaurs are giant diggers roaming around.

Dinosaurs' mouths are like gigantic caves,
Their teeth giant rocks.

Dinosaurs are huge big machines.

Brendan Conder (9)
St Basil's Primary School, Widnes

The Stars

The stars are traffic lights guiding the angels,
They are like Christmas lights twinkling up above,
They are pieces of the moon falling through the sky,
The stars are fairies flying to the sun,
They are like tiny disco balls reflecting lights to the Earth.

Bethany Rowley (10)
St Basil's Primary School, Widnes

My Family

My family is a comfy bed that I can sleep on,
It is a pillow that I can rest on,
It is a heart giving me a hug,
It is a hospital when I am sick,
It is a first-aid kit when I fall,
It is a blanket keeping me warm,
It is protection when I get hurt,
It is a school keeping me from harm,
It is a rubber if I do something wrong.

Kate Parry (9)
St Basil's Primary School, Widnes

My Family

It is helpful when I am sad,
It is a friend when I fall,
It is a helping hand,
It is a first-aid kit,
It is food when I need it,
It is a heart when I am sick,
It is a blanket I can hug,
It is caring and shares with me,
It is a teddy bear,
It is a warm house.

Nichola Fraser (9)
St Basil's Primary School, Widnes

Computer

It is a screen of imagination,
It is an information box,
It tells you things you never knew,
It is an electronic box,
It is a load of electricity,
It is a downloading small television.

Ryan Batty (9)
St Basil's Primary School, Widnes

A Football

A football is a big white balloon flying through the air,
A football needs to be a magnet to the back of the net,
A football is a circle that needs to be kicked,
A football needs to be scooped up into the air with your foot,
A football needs to be placed in the back of the net.

Matthew Harrison (9)
St Basil's Primary School, Widnes

My Family

My family is like a warm fuzzy,
My family is like a lovely giant hug and kiss.

My family is like a love heart,
My family is a lovely, hot sun.

My family is a beautiful flower in the green grass,
My family is like summer when the sun shines out.

Keiron Gordon (9)
St Basil's Primary School, Widnes

What Is A Rainbow?

It is a gallon of paint dropped from Heaven,
It is the beginning of a pot of gold,
It is a family of water and light,
It is love from around the world,
It is colours of happiness from my family,
It is comets flying everywhere,
It is dreams coming true.

Louise Coleman (9)
St Basil's Primary School, Widnes

Dragon!

Starts fires,
Never tires,
Big wings,
Never sings,
Big feet,
Lots of meat,
Never hairy,
Very scary!
He never takes a bath,
So he is never clean,
This dragon's big!
This dragon's mean!

Declan Shelley (9)
St Basil's Primary School, Widnes

My Fish

My fish is like a golden bullet shooting through water,
Its fins are like razor blades cutting through blue paper,
My fish's mouth is like a petrol lawnmower cutting grass,
Its eyes are like mini bb bullets.

Regan Mullarkey (9)
St Basil's Primary School, Widnes

Nature

Flowers glistening in the sun,
They are made out of mirror.

Flowers are swaying with the grass,
While the wind whooshes past.

Flowers are growing with the grass.

Jamie Benson (9)
St Basil's Primary School, Widnes

The Horse

It is like
A pony full of hair,
It is like a soft
Pillow, so warm,
It is like a loving person,
It is like a friendly child.

Ashley Giblin (9)
St Basil's Primary School, Widnes

Animal

It is a friendly beast,
It is a white cloth of cuddles,
It is a white friend and joy,
It is a sweet gentle cloth of love,
It is Jesus, white and soft,
It is my friend,
It is cute and white and playful.

Jordan Jones (9)
St Basil's Primary School, Widnes

Magic Senses

With my ordinary eyes I can see people watching me play football,
With my magic eyes I can see tigers and lions fighting
For a scrap of meat in the jungle.

With my ordinary nose I can smell my favourite dinner cooking,
With my magic nose I can sneeze louder than my mum shouting!
A bit loud!

With my ordinary hands I can feel my fluffy teddies even
When I am asleep,
With my magic hands I can hold up a one ton weight, very heavy!

With my ordinary tongue I can taste vanilla ice cream, yummy!
With my magic tongue I can stretch to the ice cream van
And get ice cream! Mmmmmmm!

With my ordinary ears I can hear my teacher telling us what to do next,
With my magic ears I can hear motorbikes from 10 miles away,
Ouch it hurts my ears!

Jamie Whittaker (7)
St Basil's Primary School, Widnes

Magic Senses

With my ordinary eyes I can see the teacher write on the board,
With my magic eyes I can see mermaids teaching us under the sea,
With my ordinary nose I can smell my tea sizzling in the oven,
With my magic nose I can smell my favourite food from miles away,
With my ordinary hands I can feel my pencil writing,
With my magic hands I can touch skeletons from the dead,
With my ordinary tongue I can taste my ice lolly in the
freezer getting cold,
With my magic tongue I can make my tongue touch my ears,
With my ordinary ears I can hear the teacher telling us what to do,
With my magic ears I can hear kangaroos jumping in Australia.

Andrew Lawler (7)
St Basil's Primary School, Widnes

Playtime Sounds

I can hear children
Shouting like a lion that's chasing after some meat,
Screaming like policemen chasing after you,
Making funny jokes like monkeys jumping from tree to tree.

It's very noisy!

Jordan Batty (8)
St Basil's Primary School, Widnes

Magic Senses

With my ordinary eyes I can see a dog running very fast,
With my magic eyes I can see a horse flying,
With my ordinary nose I can smell my tea ready to eat,
With my magic nose I can sneeze loudly,
With my ordinary hands I can feel the rain,
With my magic hands I can lift a table,
With my ordinary tongue I can pull tongues,
With my magic tongue I can lick the huge ice cream,
With my ordinary ears I can hear the birds singing,
With my magic ears I can hear a big crowd.

Michael Hussey (7)
St Basil's Primary School, Widnes

Matthew's Bedroom

In Matthew's bedroom he keeps . . .
Ten monkeys jumping on the bed,
Nine penguins swimming in the bath,
Eight zebras hiding under the covers,
Seven fish in the penguin's mouth,
Six dogs scaring the cat to death,
Five flies annoying my mum,
Four cheetahs jumping out the window,
Three giraffes eating the wallpaper,
Two butterflies hiding in the drawer,
One bear eating the house.

Matthew Bray (8)
St Basil's Primary School, Widnes

Callum's Bedroom

In Callum's bedroom he keeps . . .
Ten tiger's eating my bed and covers,
Nine rats hitting the window and reading,
Eight monkeys playing on FIFA Street 2 on Xbox,
Seven lions doing maths and mad science,
Six gorillas eating the window and cooking,
Five ostriches running on the ceiling,
Four penguins playing hide-and-seek,
Three chipmunks being King Kong,
Two hippos on the X Factor
And one dog doing boxing on the other animals.

Callum O'Connor (7)
St Basil's Primary School, Widnes

Jenna's Bedroom

In Jenna's bedroom she keeps . . .
Ten lions running in a race,
Nine penguins jumping about,
Eight chimpanzees eating chips,
Seven tarantulas dancing,
Six dogs eating my sister,
Five ants swimming in the bath,
Four kangaroos jumping on the bed,
Three zebras throwing nuts,
Two elephants doing ballet
And one giraffe doing pop singing.

Jenna McQuirk (7)
St Basil's Primary School, Widnes

Marcus' Bedroom

In Marcus' bedroom he keeps . . .
Ten monkeys swinging on the light bulbs,
Nine mice eating his bed covers,
Eight birds pecking on the window,
Seven fish swimming in his drink of water,
Six seals playing football,
Five lions trying to do their hair,
Four cheetahs having a race,
Three spiders climbing up the wall,
Two bears wrestling
And one hippo dancing around his bed.

Marcus Dowd (8)
St Basil's Primary School, Widnes

Mark's Bedroom

In Mark's bedroom he keeps . . .
Ten mice playing soccer,
Nine crocodiles painting hedges,
Eight flies biting cherries,
Seven spiders climbing a shower,
Six chimps playing tag,
Five bats playing basketball,
Four flies drinking milk,
Three eels playing golf,
Two fish baking cakes
And one bear playing Indians.

Mark Allen (7)
St Basil's Primary School, Widnes

Olivia's Bedroom

In Olivia's bedroom she keeps . . .
Ten giraffes eating my curtains,
Nine elephants eating my pillows,
Eight spiders crawling along my bed,
Seven seals sleeping in my bed,
Six zebras jumping on my TV,
Five penguins jumping on my window ledge,
Four rabbits dancing in my room,
Three bats juggling in my room,
Two tigers on their toes,
One lion biting me.

Olivia Hargreaves (7)
St Basil's Primary School, Widnes

Growing Up

When I was one I loved throwing my bottle on the floor,
When I was two I learnt to walk and run but I was still wobbly,
When I was three I liked to hide my dad's beer from him!
When I was four I had my picture taken on holiday,
When I was five I started school and liked it,
When I was six I went to Year 1 and got very good at my maths,
When I was seven I started table tennis and beat everyone,
Now I am eight my dad has got me a faster motorbike.

Terry Capes (8)
St Basil's Primary School, Widnes

Growing Up Poem

When I was one people used to tickle me and I would grin,
When I was two I used to scream and stamp my feet,
When I was three I used to run around in circles then fall over,
When I was four I would hide at the back of all the grown-ups,
When I was five I would always fall off my bike,
When I was six I started After School Club,
Now I am seven I can go to brownies and have fun.

Olivia Alexander (7)
St Basil's Primary School, Widnes

Growing Up Poem

When I was one I slept until I felt hungry and thirsty,
When I was two I learnt to walk but I kept on falling over,
When I was three I didn't wear nappies anymore because
I wanted to be big,
When I was four I started school and I cried so I didn't
have to go in but I still had to,
When I was five I got to learn to ride my bike on the field,
When I was six I learnt to ride my skates but I kept on falling over,
Now I am seven, I love to dance and do gymnastics.

Amy Littler (7)
St Basil's Primary School, Widnes

My Little Sister

My little sister makes me happy,
My little sister fills her nappy,
My little sister snuggles up in bed,
When she cries, her face goes red,
When her gums feel numb,
Cos her teeth have not come,
She often chews on her thumb!

My little sister sucks my nose,
When she's washed, she smells of a rose,
My little sister likes her food,
My little sister is a cool dude,
She's just been christened a while ago,
Now she's a Christian which I know.

She smiles a lot and she laughs too,
She sleeps through the night like me and you,
Her heart is like a block of gold,
She never cries though I am told,
My little sister can be a grump sometimes,
Who cares? Not me, never mind!

She's still my little skin and blister,
My one and only little sister!

Meghan O'Meara (8)
St Luke's CE Primary School, Warrington

Santa

S is for *santa* who delivers presents at Christmas,
A is for *all* the baubles you put on your Christmas tree,
N is for *nice* children who get lots of nice presents,
T is for *the* snow on top of the mountains,
A is for *all* the yummy Christmas puddings you eat.

Gemma Baron (8)
St Luke's CE Primary School, Warrington

Favourite Sandwich

I love to eat my favourite sandwich with jelly bellies
And curled up wellies,
I sometimes put in lots of hair and most of all my underwear,
I even pour in vampire blood and orange cream and
Lots and lots of dried up mud,
I grind it with lots of bugs, big fat slugs and massive rugs,
Sometimes mustard and jugs full of custard,
Rats and bats and screaming little mats.

Jake Knox (8)
St Luke's CE Primary School, Warrington

Snowman

S is for Santa
N is for naughty children not getting presents,
O is for outside carol-singers,
W is for woolly gloves,
M is for many reindeer,
A is for all Santa's supporters,
N is for nibbling Christmas mice.

Alex Cathie (8)
St Luke's CE Primary School, Warrington

Sisters Are Blisters

Sisters are blisters as you would know,
I simply just wish that they would go,
Sisters really everyone should hate,
Because for everything they make you late!

Even when I was as young as two,
I wished I could flush them down the loo,
Then when I get something new and say cool,
They just say, 'Shut up fool!'

So when I have to put up with sisters all day,
I simply just wish they would fly away.

Lizzy Lever (8)
St Luke's CE Primary School, Warrington

Snowman

S is for snow,
N is for nice children playing in the snow,
O is for outside children playing,
W is for winter snow,
M is for massive presents,
A is for all children playing with the snow,
N is for nearly all teeth chattering.

Daniel Hough (8)
St Luke's CE Primary School, Warrington

World Cup Glory

In 4 years England will be getting on the plane,
Facing countries which are hard to name,
Let's hope we win since Peter Crouch's legs have grown,
So let's all sing 'We're simply the best,
Just forget all the rest,'
Forget Brazil they will lose,
If they play England bring on the boos,
Cos England make anything possible,
Not even Owen will get an injury,
Just because England don't like hospital,
If we all sing this song,
Surely nothing will go wrong,
With shiny football boots and a
Coach who will bring us near,
Winning the World Cup would make
2010 a happy year.

Michael Donohue (8)
St Luke's CE Primary School, Warrington

Hallowe'en Night

It's Hallowe'en night I'm lying in bed,
With images of vampires flying through my head,
At twelve o'clock straight, the door gave a creak,
I swore I heard someone screaming and I gave a shriek!
The walls seemed to enclose and shut out the lamplight,
There were shivers down my spine and it gave me a fright,
The bed sheets flew off me and made a figure of a ghoul,
Please someone stop this nightmare, it's really uncool,
But as hard as I tried to get away, the more I knew it was real,
The ghoul said in an unfriendly way,
'You're going to be my midnight meal!'
By this point I was frozen with fright,
What more could go wrong on Hallowe'en night?
But just as the ghoul was going to take its first bite,
My mum came in and switched on the light,
'Oh thank goodness Mum, I'm so glad you're here!'
I said in a voice full of fright and fear,
'There was a vampire in my room,
I could swear it Mum,' and she replied,
'There's no more to be done,
The noises you heard coming into your room,
Weren't mummies or vampires coming out of their tombs,
The noises you heard in your room my sweet,
Was me banging round putting varnish on my feet!'
'Oh I'm so glad, oh Mum, Mum, Mum,
I thought a haunted house had come.'
'Now go to sleep and have sweet dreams
And don't dream of vampires but other themes!

Megan Louise Simpson (9)
St Luke's CE Primary School, Warrington

Football Crazy, Football Mad

Football crazy, football mad, I am a good footballer, not bad,
I play for a team and we never scream when the ball hits our head,
When I score a goal I celebrate near a pole
And I think that gives me good luck,
Now I play football, I can never stop,
I can score a goal, I can hit the jackpot.

James Cathie (8)
St Luke's CE Primary School, Warrington

Winter

W inter, winter,
I s so great,
N o more sun so keep the snow,
T he snowball fight is such a brilliant game,
E nd of winter is such a shame,
R ush back round, and come again.

Lewis Stones (8)
St Luke's CE Primary School, Warrington

Hallowe'en

On Hallowe'en in the night,
There are lots of frights.

Some people egg your house,
It's scarier than a mouse.

There are no lights,
So you'll get lots of frights.

You'll get hit by a car,
That will knock you far.

Remember you'll get lots of treats,
But there's some kind of meats.

Dylan Lowe (9)
St Luke's CE Primary School, Warrington

The Haunted Hallowe'en House

This house is crooked and old,
This is a poem never to be told,
This is a house scary and dark,
If you go in, you will hear the dog bark,
If you go in the cupboard you will see a bat,
If you go in the kitchen you will see a witch
That will squash you flat.

Kate Sutcliffe-Ralph (8)
St Luke's CE Primary School, Warrington

My Classroom

I noticed chairs moving back and forth,
Until I heard the door slam into the classroom wall,
I watched the lights flicker on and off
And I saw a ghost come out of the loft,
Then I felt a breath run down my back,
I stared at the pens moving up and down,
I crammed under the table when the projector fell,
I tried to get out, it was impossible,
I darted around to get out of the dark, scary classroom.

Hayley Tait (10)
St Luke's CE Primary School, Warrington

True Story

This morning I jumped into my aeroplane
And went out to fly,
Then my radar started beeping
And an eagle flew by,
It smashed into my engine,
As it let out a lot of heat,
Red alert, red alert, red alert,
Then up in my ejector seat,
I flew up, up, up,
Into the air
And saw a little green alien,
Who didn't half stare!

Edward Hanley (11)
St Luke's CE Primary School, Warrington

What Is Yellow?

(Based on 'What is Pink?' by Christina Rossetti)

What is yellow? The sun is yellow,
Beaming bright and mellow.
What is white? A cloud is white,
Soft enough to take a bite.
What is blue? The ocean is blue,
With little fish floating through.
What is gold? A star is gold,
Big, round, bright and bold.
What is pink? Pigs are pink,
They sit in your kitchen sink.
What is red? Poppies are red,
Sitting in your flower bed.
What is green? Leaves are green,
With branches in-between.
What is black? Rabbits are black,
The colour of a black sack.
What is orange? A goldfish is orange,
Bobbing in its bowl.
What is purple? Heather is purple,
Purple heather on a hill.
What is brown? A chocolate bar is brown,
You buy it when you go into town.

Abigail Gibson (10)
St Luke's CE Primary School, Warrington

My Classroom

I heard an eerie child's voice laughing,
I watched the cupboard doors slowly opening and shutting,
I discovered a skull in a drawer, its deformed face looked at me,
I heard a heartbeat from inside the wall,
I felt all of the painting's eyes watching me.

Tommy Isherwood (9)
St Luke's CE Primary School, Warrington

My Classroom

I saw the pen writing on the whiteboard,
'St Luke's' over and over again,
I saw the table rattling as I gazed around in shock,
I heard a voice in the cloakroom, it sounded like screaming people,
I heard footsteps coming closer and closer,
As I stood as if I was frozen,
I discovered that gloopy slimy slugs came out of a wall in one corner,
I noticed that the laptop was moving every time I moved an arm,
I heard the door knock, I went to the door
And held out my hand and that was that . . .

Ashley Hough (10)
St Luke's CE Primary School, Warrington

What Is Green?

(Based on 'What is Pink?' by Christina Rossetti)

What is green?
The grass is green,
Swaying through the wintry scene.
What is pink?
A pig is pink sitting in the sink.
What is yellow?
A sun is yellow, like a little happy fellow.
What is black?
The sky is black, like a big black sack.
What is blue?
The sky is blue, swaying through.
What is red?
A heart is red, snuggled in my bed.

Ashley Hughes (11)
St Luke's CE Primary School, Warrington

The Typical North West

Above, above,
Rain clouds on the Pennines.

Below, below,
The rain drains away.

Side to side,
Tall buildings and council houses.

Sea to sea,
Stormy seas and shipwrecks.

Tree to tree,
A wet muddy park with loads of rubbish.

Duncan Cathie (10)
St Luke's CE Primary School, Warrington

Stars

Look at the stars, they shine so bright,
In the darkness of the night,
Some are laughing, some are crying,
Some are whining, but they're all,
Shining, shining, shining through the night.

Look at the moon and sun,
Having lots of fun,
Flying at the horrible height,
Making such a pretty sight,
They're shining, shining, shining,
Owwww my eye!

Lorrna Allison (10)
St Luke's CE Primary School, Warrington

What Is Pink?

(Based on 'What is Pink?' by Christina Rossetti)

What is pink? Dresses are pink,
Dancing in an ice rink.
What is blue? The sea is blue,
Floating all the way through.
What is yellow? A banana is yellow,
Smooth and soft and mellow.
What is violet? The sky is violet,
In the sky twilight.
What is green? The grass is green,
In a beautiful scene.
What is red? A rose is red,
In a grassy flower bed.
What is orange? My sister's fringe is orange,
Straight and long, well it's just orange.
What is black? A back sack's black,
On my dad's back.
What is white? A ghost is white,
In the darkness of the night.

Jessica Smart (10)
St Luke's CE Primary School, Warrington

My Classroom!

I could smell the strong smell of petrol coming from the corner,
I saw the maths display, hanging off the display board,
I heard the main door creaking as it went back and forth,
I felt the freezing radiator, as it froze my body still,
I discovered the moving blinds, swaying in the wind,
I noticed the chairs had disappeared, as if they were never there,
I listened carefully to the wind, whistling in the playground,
I watched the papers flying around the classroom,
I touched the whiteboard, shivering with fear and fright,
I sensed a presence near me, as though it needed my help . . .

Alice Grix (10)
St Luke's CE Primary School, Warrington

My Classroom

I saw a chair shuffle across the floor of the classroom,
I discovered that the wall was crumbling in on me,
I heard the projector buzzing down my ear,
I felt a cold breeze swirling down my spine,
I noticed the door was hanging in a very odd way,
I gasped as the paper began to fly round the room,
I watched as the lights flickered on and off
But they never managed to stay on,
I was amazed as the blinds opened and closed
With no one there,
I cried as someone muttered down my ear,
But there was no one there . . .

Laura Marston (10)
St Luke's CE Primary School, Warrington

My Classroom

I saw the lights flicker on and off,
So I put them on fully,
I noticed the walls ooze with goo,
I tried to clean it up,
I discovered the chalkboard screeched,
I covered my ears,
I heard the doors creak open,
I ran through the door and locked it,
I felt blood drop from the sky,
I put my hood up,
I reached because something brushed my leg,
I thought it tickled.

Alex Bradbury (10)
St Luke's CE Primary School, Warrington

Winter

Winter is freezing weather,
Cold and very wet,
Winter is snowy,
As it falls on your head,
Winter is for going sledging,
Down snowy and damp hills,
Winter is for singing,
To all your neighbours,
Winter is for Santa coming,
Bringing you some presents,
Winter is Christmas trees,
Green and very prickly.

Beth Davies (10)
St Luke's CE Primary School, Warrington

Packing Up For Our Holidays

When we're packing up for our holidays,
It gets into a fight
And everyone starts to row
And we punch with all our might.

When we're packing up for our holidays,
It always gets out of hand
And everyone starts to shout
And Mother always takes command.

When we're packing up for our holidays,
It gets a little mad
And when we land at our destination,
Everyone's very glad.

Alex Corcoran (10)
St Luke's CE Primary School, Warrington

My Classroom

I discovered that the window was smashed in and the wind gushed in,
I heard the door slam shut, I jumped with fright when I heard it,
I shook as I felt cold hands touch my back,
Then I stood still and watched the desk crash into nothing on the floor,
I cried with fright when I saw the chairs rolling around the room,
I heard people whispering in my ear, but I don't know if I was
Imagining it or not,
I gasped as an ice-cold ice cube dropped down my back,
I watched my pencil case fall off the table and all the stationery fall out,
I noticed that the projector was flicking on and off with no one there,
I dropped to my knees and cried as I left the room.

Annabelle Coveney (10)
St Luke's CE Primary School, Warrington

My Classroom

I felt a chilling breeze,
Dangerously close,
I saw the whiteboard,
Flickering on and off,
Spookily constant.

I noticed chairs dancing,
Spritely across the room,
I sensed a ghostly presence,
Spritely making itself known.

I wondered why the phone rang
And nobody was there,
I thought I saw a ghostly face,
Sadly looking upon me.

I tried to shut out the spookiness,
But the images just kept coming in,
I feared that this classroom,
Was going to be my last.

I discovered that old bones,
Were piled up bloodily under a desk,
I pretended that I wasn't here,
But my mind was not capable.

I clambered up to leave,
But spirits just pulled me back in,
I gasped for air,
As spirits were taking my breath,
This is my last moment . . .

Ben Graney (10)
St Luke's CE Primary School, Warrington

My Classroom

I saw the number grid, it was still there,
The numbers were coming out of the plastic pockets,
The books were flying round in the air,
Why though, I do not know,
I felt shivery whilst the wind blew at me,
I heard something, I turned round and looked,
At the French display,
The H fell off, the C fell off, the N fell off,
The E fell off, the R fell off, then the F,
I discovered that the chairs were rocking and rolling,
All over the place, I did not know what was going on,
I looked at the clock because it was ticking, ticking and ticking,
I realised the second time I looked at it, it was vanishing,
I still felt cold, then I felt my classroom had gone freaky,
I noticed the walls turned cream to black with spiders' webs,
I was astonished that my classroom had turned into a
Haunted house, I thought it was my imagination but it wasn't,
My heart was beating very fast.

Kathryn Gildart (10)
St Luke's CE Primary School, Warrington

Demons In The Night

When everyone is fast asleep
And tucked away in bed,
Demons come to kill and reap,
Their eyes are fiery red.

They enter your room,
As you're snoring loud,
To put you to doom,
Would make them so proud.

They party around,
In the shadows of the night
And when you're awake,
They give you such fright.

As morning draws near,
They retreat to their home,
A land of fear,
Where they all sleep alone.

Jack Hamilton (10)
St Luke's CE Primary School, Warrington

Xmas Row

Snowflakes falling from the sky,
Big roaring fires and apple pie,
Hearing the bell go ding-dong,
Carol-singers at the door,
They keep coming more and more,
On Christmas Day everyone's happy,
Mum and Dad are glad everyone's OK
Until . . .
The kids start to row about
Who has the most
One starts crying, the other boasts,
Mum and Dad try their best,
To get out of this mess,
Dong goes the bell, in come the family,
The fight is forgotten
And all are happy.

Aidan McMenemy (11)
St Luke's CE Primary School, Warrington

Wintertime

Winter is a time of fun
And seeing lots of snow.

Winter is freezing cold
And lots of hats and scarves.

Winter is snowflakes
And lots of crunching noises.

Winter is Christmas time
And lots of carol singers.

Winter is Christmas trees
And bright with lots of light.

Elle Hart (11)
St Luke's CE Primary School, Warrington

My Classroom

I saw the light vanish as the bulb shattered,
I heard the door creaking as it opened and shut,
I noticed that the whiteboard was waiting,
Do not leave!
I discovered that the clock was on midnight
And stayed,
I saw the pictures' eyes gaze at me,
I was feeling so, so scared, I almost died of fright.

Josh Taylor (10)
St Luke's CE Primary School, Warrington

My Classroom

I felt James' names on the blackboard drip on my face like blood,
I discovered spiders coming out of the carpet,
I heard the door creaking, my ears were in pain,
I saw the chairs breaking into little bits,
I noticed the clock was not working,
I watched the blinds fall down,
I noticed the lights flashing on and off,
I discovered the smart board was not working
I saw the words of the week disappear.

George Lythgoe (10)
St Luke's CE Primary School, Warrington

My Classroom

I heard the sound of a door slam,
I noticed writing dripping from the white board,
Forming a red pool on the floor,
I felt a cold hand climbing up my spine, I stood dead,
I saw the lights switching, clicking on and off,
Then the lights didn't come on, I saw glowing eyes,
I noticed that the window was open,
The curtains were ripped but they weren't before,
I heard a cackle next door, I reached for the door
But I daren't go in,
I witnessed the chairs stacking themselves,
I tried to make a run for it but
I got hung up by the skipping ropes,
I shouted for help but I just heard a voice shout,
'I will get revenge you will see!'

Mark Harrison
St Luke's CE Primary School, Warrington

Star Wars

The Republic is crumbling,
Just like some cake,
Along with the Jedi,
Just by a simple mistake.

Because of stupid Anakin,
That big dope,
Here comes Darth Vader,
In 'The New Hope.'

Back in the past,
When the Jedi did rule,
The Dark Side was really,
Heading to drool.

Because of the death,
Of Taranus and Fett,
This is the story,
You will never forget.

Now down goes Maul
And Grievous too,
Obi-Wan killed both,
But not Mace Windu.

It's hard to believe,
But the light side had won!
Those troopers were all dead,
When that happened. ..
The war was done!

Xaq Atkins (8)
St Luke's CE Primary School, Warrington

Hallowe'en Dream

H is for haunted, creeping around,
A is for ace Hallowe'en party,
L is for lying in bed at night,
L is for light turned on,
O is for 'Oh no' in a devil's lair,
W is for wicked, a witch's night,
E is for evil magic at the end of the day,
E is for eight o'clock at night,
N is for night, end of the day.

Amy Bradford (7)
St Luke's CE Primary School, Warrington

The Wind

He flew across the old crowded city,
Trashing cars on top of each other,
Blowing tiles off roofs as he flew over them,
Then he started to throw dustbins at people,
He went up to a wrestler and blew at him with all his might,
But he didn't fall over because he was on the run,
He didn't like the people and he blew them about,
He played tricks on people especially old ones,
He ruined people's lives and made them run
Away until nothing was left,
He ran off sulking because nothing was left,
Then a city caught the corner of his eye,
For him to destroy again.

Josh Walley (10)
Sir John Offley CE (VC) Primary School

The Storm

He dashed around and up and down,
He whirled up dashing at a balloon upsetting a girl,
Sprinting through the dusk turns up and around.

What was in his way?
Quickly twisting around and around corners,
Picking up cars and using them as boomerangs,
Thunder bounces off rooftops and frightens
Everybody in town,
Clashing into people,
Pinching them on the arms,
Howling through people's cars like alarms.

Jumping roof to roof looking like a rock star,
Throwing tiles pretending they are autographs,
Triumphantly whizzing through people's ears,
Leaving their brain cells behind belting around and
Vandalising homes,
Lifting homes from off the ground
And now he's winding down.

Jack Allport (10)
Sir John Offley CE (VC) Primary School

The Sun

He rises bright and early,
Opens his eyes and beams,
He shines his almighty light,
In the clear blue sky,
Then starts to paint people red,
Playing hide-and-seek with the clouds,
Then paints shadows on the ground,
He goes down the rainbow with colour all round,
He goes down from the sky,
Then goes into the darkest night.

George Edwards (11)
Sir John Offley CE (VC) Primary School

Storm

He blew a hat off an old man,
He sprinted down the crusty road
And he collected wood to make a fire
And crashed into a tree on his way,
He crashed into homes and blew old trees and people
And put prints on the cars,
Making fires all around him and
Playing bending cars and playing football with them.

Liam Jennings (10)
Sir John Offley CE (VC) Primary School

The Sun

He wakes up bright and early
And meets his friend Cloud,
Spraying people red and brown
While their skin is peeling off their arms,
He has a beaming smile on his face,
Sprinting down the rainbow like it's a slide,
Then swallows thousands of gulps of water,
He happily walks quickly across the sky,
He is so bright, he is blinding people below,
He looks down at people below
And prints shadows and shines for everyone to see,
Night comes and he plays with his friend Moon,
Then he goes to bed.

Eleasha Baddeley (10)
Sir John Offley CE (VC) Primary School

The Wind

He started to stamp loudly crushing the things underneath him,
Smashing windows as he was going past them,
Quickly and powerful, he lifted up cars,
Throwing them at people then quickly running off,
He peeked behind people and pinched their hats,
Playing jokes on them, fast and sneaky,
Storming down dustbins blowing litter around,
Being very, very naughty.

Then he started to calm down as if going to sleep,
Flowing across gardens slowly and peacefully,
He tiptoed to children and played with them gently,
Rolling in the air quietly turning round and round,
He was going up in the air to calmly go to sleep.

Bethany Lewis (11)
Sir John Offley CE (VC) Primary School

The Sun

She wakes up bright and early,
Her shimmering hair dangling,
She disappears behind the clouds,
Playing hide-and-seek,
Wraps her arms around people,
Cuddling them with her warmth,
Sprinting down the slippery rainbow,
Evaporating the sea water,
She starts blinding people with her beauty,
Dusk comes and she plays with the moon,
She gets angry when the clouds cover her.

Keely Bagnall (10)
Sir John Offley CE (VC) Primary School

The Rain

She starts by watering the gardens,
But that never takes very long,
She adores giving people showers,
But not when they stick out their tongue!

She is a really great joker,
But people don't enjoy her jokes,
Children run in squealing and shrieking,
But some only put on their coats.

And when it's the end of the day,
She goes noiselessly away,
But she will be back again,
Probably the very next day!

Elizabeth Courthold (10)
Sir John Offley CE (VC) Primary School

Wind

He started attacking his prey,
Punching and kicking and screaming,
He did all of this damage but he had no meaning,
He huffed and puffed,
Blew and blew,
He stampeded up the hill,
Getting ready for the kill,
Suddenly he froze, his anger was melting.

Automatically he started drifting,
Floating elegantly down the hill,
He got to the bottom by rolling beautifully,
He started playing with the sea,
Giggling gently and calmly,
Then he jumped up in alarm
And stroked the top of my relaxed head,
Then curled up and went to his world, bed.

Hannah Beardmore (10)
Sir John Offley CE (VC) Primary School

The Wind

He whirled around smashing windows,
Overturning cars and stealing hats,
Screaming through streets,
Making enough noise to wake up all the cats,
He climbed viciously up the buildings,
Menacingly howling,
Frightening people violently growling,
Swooping around and pulling houses down.

He gently walked through people's ears,
Tiptoeing slowly around,
Whispering peacefully making no sound,
Drifting gently doing no harm,
The sun came out but he stayed there,
Hovering around without a care.

Kate Valentine (10)
Sir John Offley CE (VC) Primary School

The Rain

He rolls off roofs,
Getting people all wet,
Springing into the puddles,
Making the puddles upset.

Beating down just like drums,
Striking water on people and cars,
Shoots up to space, getting aliens wet
And falling back down from Mars.

He's finally finished,
Because the sun has come out,
Now what was that rain
All about?

Eleni Caulcott (10)
Sir John Offley CE (VC) Primary School

The Sun

She wakes up bright and early
And opens her eyes and shimmers,
Her burning body of fire,
Sprays people red and brown,
She loves to go on holiday
And travels the world in a day,
She blinds people as they drive,
Sucking up puddles on her way,
She prints shadows on the ground,
Playing with the rainbow,
Dodging clouds in the gorgeous sky,
Shining down on the ground,
Now it's time to go to bed,
She is very sad,
Let's swap with the moon
And then we're up again.

Sophie Key (10)
Sir John Offley CE (VC) Primary School

The Storm

He galloped through the deserted roads,
Gnashing his teeth as he flew,
Dodging cars at a furious pace,
Punching people across the face,
Lifting climbing frames,
He bulldozed dustbins fuming and angry,
Gritting his teeth,
He started to pant and slow down,
All across the towns.

Lucy Prall (10)
Sir John Offley CE (VC) Primary School

Sun

He wakes up bright and early,
He yawns and stretches wide,
Sprays people brown causing peeling skin,
His beaming eyes blinding people in their cars,
He sprints across the clear blue sky,
Evaporating water with his almighty strength,
Playing hide-and-seek with the clouds,
Blinding people with his vigorous eyes,
He paints shadows on the burning ground,
He sprints through the crowded clouds.

Thomas Hedley (10)
Sir John Offley CE (VC) Primary School

The Rain

He drops bombs in human's faces,
While banging on people's windowpanes,
Coming down at supersonic paces,
Bullying people and becoming a pain,
He sings a song as he hits the path,
Pitter-patter he goes,
But then he comes down softly
And pats people on their head,
He does this before he dies out
And before he goes to bed,
He lies on the pavement, no movement at all
And waits to evaporate till there's nothing left at all.

Dan Brown (10)
Sir John Offley CE (VC) Primary School

The Storm

He sprinted through the enormous mud fields,
Smashing all the cars,
Dancing and prancing up on the mud tracks,
Twisting and turning,
Gnashing his teeth and shaking the trees.

Jade Ellerton (10)
Sir John Offley CE (VC) Primary School

The Storm

He whooshed across the rough city,
Smashed and crashed over buildings,
Lifting the top off buildings, he threw cars everywhere
And would not stop,
He stamped on houses viciously,
People flying into trees,
Then suddenly the people stopped flying into trees,
Cars stopped flying everywhere,
He got worn out and he was calming down,
Trees stopped flying,
Phew, I thought I was going to get stamped on by the storm.

Tom Law (10)
Sir John Offley CE (VC) Primary School

The Wind

I elegantly jogged through gardens and fields,
My arms moved with the gentle breeze
And slowly he rushed into fuming angry mode,
I screamed like a banshee
And kicked dustbins and cars,
In my terrible bad-mannered temper screaming and yelling
And suddenly I turned back into a calm angelic angel,
I drifted back through gardens and fields,
Singing quietly and jogged when the sun came out,
The power was all on me,
I felt sweet and pretty but then the wind,
Died out!
I snuggled off to my warm cosy bed.

Rebecca Machin (10)
Sir John Offley CE (VC) Primary School

Sun

She wakes up every morning,
Shining in the sky,
Opens her eyes and suddenly,
People below are burning,
At 10 o'clock she gets ready for work,
Then she gets to work
Wrapping you in her long stretchy arms of warmth,
She bobs along the sky printing
Shadows where she wants,
Shining and shimmering, swishing
Her long golden hair, blowing a warm breeze,
It is half-past three and all the children
Are enjoying the warmth,
She travels around the world,
She can do it in a day,
But dusk has come,
She is ready to sleep and wait for dawn the next day.

Danielle Riley (10)
Sir John Offley CE (VC) Primary School

What's In Your Mouth?

Bubblegum (yummy)
A rubber (mmm tasty)
A pencil lead (tastes leadish)
A tyre (tastes rubbery)
A chair leg (tastes metally)

Stay in at playtime,
Have detention,
Save your excuses for the headmaster.

A book (tastes treeish)
A jumper (tastes cottony)
A ruler (tastes plasticky)
Hair (tastes stringy)
Ink (tastes inky).

Sam Scott (10)
Tilston Parochial CE Primary School

Why Aren't You Doing PE?

Because I have got a poorly tummy,
Because I have got a poorly finger,
Because I have got a sprained ankle,
Because I have broken my arm,
Because I am in *hospital,*
I mean, I forgot my PE kit.

Megan Adie (9)
Tilston Parochial CE Primary School

What's In Your Pocket Girl?

My best pink doll,
An empty can,
Two pieces of bubblegum,
A pair of earrings,
A floppy dog.

What are you hiding?
What is it?
What are you hiding girl?

A piece of cheese,
A car,
An African bunny,
A ball,
Eight hair bobbles,
A wizard.

What are you hiding?
What is it?
What are you hiding girl?

What?

Aimee Foden (10)
Tilston Parochial CE Primary School

What's In Your Pocket?

Teacher repellent!
A nuclear bomb!
A magic three-eyed hamster named Maisy!
The whole of Canada!
I mean . . . nothing!

It can't be that!
Tell me the truth!
What are you hiding?
What are you hiding?
What are you hiding today?

A giant cheese sculpture of a reindeer!
A purple frog!
One hundred pounds!
A ten-foot three-headed dragon!
I mean . . . nothing!

It can't be that!
Tell me the truth!
What are you hiding?
What are you hiding?
Oh no, there goes the bell!

Ruby Doran (10)
Tilston Parochial CE Primary School

It Wasn't Me!

Who put the dog in the dishwasher?
It wasn't me,
It was Bob!
He came round to my house to play with me,
But he wasn't nice, he broke my toys, called me names
And blamed me when he broke the TV . . .
And then to make things worse . . .
He put my fluffy, cute, silly dog Bracken in the dishwasher,
Then he blamed me!
It's just *not fair!*

Who flooded the bathroom?
It wasn't me,
It was Ted!
He was sleeping at my house and he went to brush his teeth,
He put the taps on full blast,
When I got up in the morning to wash my face,
There was a tidal wave and it hit me in the face . . .
And then he *blamed me,*
It's just not fair!

Henry Delf-Rowlandson (10)
Tilston Parochial CE Primary School

What's In Your Secret Box?

A piece of chewing gum,
Tell me what else boy, tell me what else?
An Indian elephant,
Tell me what else boy, tell me what else?
A Mercedes clicky,
Tell me what else boy, tell me what else?
20 tonnes of Lego,
Tell me what else boy, tell me what else?
I've got the key to the world,
Tell me what else boy, tell me what else?
I've got a state of the art laptop,
Tell me what else boy, tell me what else?
A sniper rifle,
Tell me what else boy, tell me what else?
I mean, nothing Sir.

Andrew Ewins (10)
Tilston Parochial CE Primary School

Why Didn't You Print Your Work Out?

The printer died,
It was evil!
It turned out to be a mad printer!
I stuck a broom down its throat!
The *paper attacked me!*
It jumped off the school roof,
It swallowed me and spat me out again,
That's how I got these tattoos!
There wasn't any paper!

Nonsense!
That's pathetic,
Save your excuses until playtime.

Hang on a minute, I thought you said there wasn't any paper,
There wasn't any paper after *it attacked me!*

Liam Cork (8)
Tilston Parochial CE Primary School

Our Garden Hippo

We have a hippopotamus at the bottom of our garden,
He's waiting for his friends, for them to come and play.

They all jumped into the pond, they did,
They all jumped into the pond.

There's Ryan the rhino, there's Fiona the frog,
There's Toby the turtle, there's Dotty the dog,
Last came Poppy the poodle and Eddy the elephant.

They all jumped into the pond, they did,
They all jumped into the pond.

They all jumped in with a shout, 'What's happened,
The water's all out?'

They all jumped into the pond, they did,
They all jumped into the pond.

Lydia Ewins (8)
Tilston Parochial CE Primary School

What's In Your Pocket Boy?

A Game Boy,
A water pistol,
A paper clip,
Some humbugs.

You're not allowed that
What!

A pencil,
Two cinema tickets,
Three stones,
Four stink bombs.

You're now allowed that
What!

A mini TV,
A CBBC goodie,
Two fake rats
And finally a pea shooter.

Liam Griffiths (11)
Tilston Parochial CE Primary School

Wasn't Meee

Mum, Mum, it wasn't me,
Dad, Dad, it wasn't me,
Wasn't me, wasn't me, wasn't me, whatever!

Who took the rat out of its cage and let it go?
Who strangled the guinea pig with a yo-yo?
Who hung the baby on the washing line by its ears?
Who fed the rabbit burger and chips?

Mum, Mum, it wasn't me,
Dad, Dad, it wasn't me,
Wasn't me, wasn't me, wasn't me, whatever!

Who stole the budgie from the pet shop?
Who painted the dog in purple spots?
Who put the cat in the washing machine?
Who shaved the fur off the hamster?

Mum, Mum, it wasn't me,
Dad, Dad, it wasn't me,
Wasn't me, wasn't me, wasn't me, whatever!
It was you, I'm telling!

Lauren McGann (9)
Tilston Parochial CE Primary School

What's In Your Pocket?

Well, what's in your pocket boy?
It's an empty drinks carton, Miss.

Well, that's not good enough,
I shall be seeing you tonight.

Well, what's in your pocket hey?
I have a sticky sweet covered in fluff,
A mouldy piece of cheese and a snapped pencil!

Well, that's not good enough,
I shall be seeing you tonight.

Well, what's in your pocket?
It's a sticky green freebie which is not sticky anymore
And eyes lost but I still like it and I've got a
Teddy bear that all the stuffing's coming out of!

Well, that's not good enough,
I shall be seeing you tonight!

Well, what's in your pocket girl?
Well, it's a friendship bracelet and a piece of gum!

Well, that's not good enough,
I shall be seeing you tonight.

I will be looking forward to seeing you all tonight.

Lizzie Hunter (10)
Tilston Parochial CE Primary School